Hi & Bye

Inhale Peace, Exhale Stress

Nyla Barnes

ISBN 978-1-7377883-9-3

Printed in the USA
Published by SIP Publications, LLC and Junior Authors
Designed by 5.13 Graphics & Media, LLC
www.thejuniorauthors.com

Acknowledgments

I want to shout out one of my closest friends, Ari Johnson. Thank you for helping me with the book in the early stages. You are truly amazing, and I wish you many blessings in your life.

Thank you, to my Mom, Dad and my older brother Donovan for supporting me throughout this whole process. Thank you for pushing me to keep writing even when I was tired or didn't have the energy. I love you all very much, even when I don't show it. Thank you, Nana and Papa, for your love and support. My appreciation will never be shown as big as I want it to be. I especially want to thank the Junior Authors program, for allowing me this opportunity to follow my passion.

Without everyone's love, compassion, and support, my book wouldn't exist. Thank you Mom for listening to my dreams and helping this one come true, I am very grateful. I'm very excited to see what I write next!

Table of Contents

Introduction

'Hi & Bye' is a book specifically written for teens and young people. I thought about all of the people who might be struggling to let something go or having trouble bringing light into their dark situation. I chose 'Hi & Bye' as my title because it's simple yet powerful.

The "Hi" part of my title represents what I am introducing or mentioning. The "hi" also introduces new and optimistic things to do or see. It's like when you see your new neighbor moving in across the street, you want to introduce yourself to them and the neighborhood. You might want to tell them about the annual events that make their neighborhood the best. Each word from my 'hi' list is meant to help you with anything delightful in your life. Of course, there are tons of options out there, however, I think these are the ones that are probably the simplest, most convenient ways that most people can do.

Maybe you feel your life is all together, but maybe you have a friend or relative that could use some help. By trying these recommendations, they can possibly see improvements during the process. They may even discover a new hobby or habit that they may come to deeply enjoy.

The "Bye" part of my title represents all of the different types of "dead weight" that need to be cut out of your life. Disappointment, hate, disruption, and pessimistic thoughts need to be erased from your life, step-by-step. It might be frustrating to let go, but imagine it as a heavyweight being lifted off your shoulders. You'll feel relief & hopefully, some balance and peace.

Each word from my 'Bye' list is an example that describes obstructive events that might be happening in your life right now. Some of the biggest problems might be stress, anxiety, depression, or family issues. This may not be a big deal to one person, but to another person, it's the issue that has been causing them not to have the life they're desiring. It's important to respect whatever a person is going through because you have no idea what it's like until you walk in their shoes.

Maybe with a different perspective, you can look at it as if you're achieving a goal. You might have a bad habit of biting your nails, for example. It's something you don't wish to continue, so you make it a goal to stop those bad habits and to start healthy habits instead. It's a great thing to create goals because it encourages you to begin a healthier lifestyle

I have enjoyed thinking about what special messages and words of advice need to be in the book. In each chapter, there will be stories; it's my way of expressing emotions, looking at different situations that hopefully people can relate to.

Ch 1. - Music + Stress

Hi~ Music: Verbal or instrumental sounds (or both) combined in such a way as to produce beauty of form, harmony, & expression of emotion.

Bye~ Stress: Pressure or tension exerted on a material object.

-A state of mental or emotional strain or tension from adverse or very demanding circumstances.

Music is a tool that can get you going for the day. When you listen to music, it can make you feel excited or happy. It can also give you the freedom to express your emotions. Honestly, some music can sound depressing, and that's what you don't need. Choose music that gives you a boost of energy, makes you dance, gives you a boost of confidence, or joy.

Stress on the other hand isn't an emotion you want to deal with or be around. Stress is caused by many things. For example, you can be stressed out by a certain homework assignment or deciding between going to one college or the other. There are many ways to relieve that stress. You just have to experiment with different ways to see which one works for you.

I would recommend taking breaks and doing breathing exercises while listening to music. Also, stress can be on different levels. There's normal stress that everyone feels like, which shirt goes best with your favorite pair of jeans? Then, there is this heavy, overwhelming type of stress. It usually comes from more serious situations like losing a family member.

My way of expressing different emotions is through stories, meet **Kayla~**

Kayla Smith is 17 years old and she lives in Houston, Texas. Her parents have been divorced since Kayla was 6, and she lives with her mom & stepdad. She goes to Eastwood High School where she has a lot of friends. Kayla has 3 best friends, Amber, Keisha, and Sariyah. It seems like her life is wonderful and filled with nothing but happiness. Even though she has her BFFs at school, she's still stressed out!

Kayla recently found out that her migraines are due to a brain tumor, and she has to get an MRI scan every two weeks because the tumor is very aggressive, so the neurosurgeons have to make sure it isn't growing. Each appointment takes up a whole school day. The doctors always ask her and her mom a bunch of questions to see if her behavior has changed, or if anything unusual is going on.

Every time she has a doctor's appointment, she falls behind in her schoolwork. Her teachers know about her brain tumor, and they try their best to minimize the amount of work for her. However, sometimes the amount of work she has to do builds up so fast that she struggles to keep up.

Kayla, Amber, Keisha, and Sariyah have all their classes together so they're able to help Kayla when she falls behind. They know about her brain tumor, the doctor appointments, and they pray for her every day. Keisha is the "brains" of the group, so she helps out Kayla the most.

Even though Kayla's teachers reduce her work as much as possible, she receives help from her friends and her parents but she's still stressed out. She has everything to help her with her stress: breathing exercises, journaling, and a therapist. However, the one tool that helps Kayla the most has been music.

Amber was the one who introduced music to Kayla and ever since then, it has been smooth sailing. Music has this calming wave in it, and when she presses that play button, all of her stress just fades away.

There are many ways to help reduce your stress, but I chose music because music calms me down and gives me peace of mind. It has this appealing vibe where I can sing along, vibe, and just feel like nothing else is important at that moment. I encourage you to try music if you haven't yet. It also doesn't matter what type of music you pick to play; just choose a style that you enjoy listening to.

MUSIC LIST:

_____

_____

_____

_____

_____

_____

_____

_____

_____

Ch 2. - Cozy Blankets + Anxiety

Hi~ Cozy Blanket: A large piece of woolen or similar material used as a bed covering or other covering for warmth.

Bye~ Anxiety: A feeling of worry, nervousness, or unease, typically about an imminent event or something with an uncertain outcome.

You should invest in your needs, and this could mean cozy blankets! People sleep best in temperatures- 60°F-67°F (15.6°C-19.4°C). Cozy blankets can represent a great memory in your life. My cozy blanket is my best friend, which keeps me warm and calms my nerves. Let's just say I have about 3.

Anxiety can be caused by pessimistic events, or by terrible dreams. There are multiple types of anxiety. You can have social anxiety, a panic disorder, OCD, and more. If you want the help you need, it'll take time, patience, and it won't be a simple process. You'll have to complete the fight in baby steps. Just remember, if you ever feel overwhelmed or pressured to do anything you don't want to do, you can say no or wait until you're ready.

A girl & her blanket~

Alyssa is 13 years old; she lives in Los Angeles, California, with her 3 siblings: 2 younger brothers who are twins, and 1 older sister. Her parents passed away 4 years ago on her birthday. They died in a car accident. Alyssa and her siblings live with their aunt and uncle. Unfortunately,

Alyssa has suffered from PTSD since she was 9 after the car accident took place.

Post-traumatic stress disorder (PTSD) is a disorder that develops in some people who have experienced a shocking, scary, or dangerous event. It is natural to feel afraid during and after a traumatic situation. Fear triggers many split-second changes in the body to help defend against danger or to avoid it.

Her aunt is a preschool teacher. However, she doesn't earn enough money to make an appointment with the doctor consistently, to see how they can help Alyssa. Her uncle is a police officer. His money helps out some, but, unfortunately, it's not enough.

Her older sister, Kamala has a job at a local restaurant to contribute towards Alyssa's doctor appointments and medication. Alyssa feels terrible. She believes that her mental disorder isn't something Kamala shouldn't have to worry about. She wants her older sister to have a normal teen life. She wants her to hang out with her friends, and just enjoy herself as much as she can but Kalama is more concerned about her little sister.

Alyssa's cozy blankets calm her, helping her with anxiety. She has had her favorite blanket since she was 2. It's lavender with her name embroidered in teal. Her mom got it custom-made for her 2nd birthday. Lately, she has been playing the video of her 2nd birthday party, and often cries when she hears her mother's voice, "Alyssa, make sure you never lose this blanket because it will become one of your most precious possessions."

Ever since then, she doesn't let anyone; I mean ANYONE touch her blanket. Alyssa is the only one that washes the blanket. She washes it in lavender scent beads because lavender is her favorite scent. Her mom would light lavender candles every Saturday for Alyssa. Alyssa can feel her mother's spirit in her blanket. She knows her parents are watching over her all the time.

I don't have PTSD, but sometimes, I can feel anxious, and when I just wrap myself around in a warm, cozy blanket, I feel my heartbeat slowing down. I love knowing one heartwarming activity or accomplishment helps me to relax, and the same thing can happen to you. So, the next time you feel your anxiety is creeping up, try wrapping up in a nice cozy warm blanket.

Ch 3. - Home-Cooked Meal + Low Confidence

Hi~ Home-Cooked Meal: Any of the regular occasions in a day when a reasonably large amount of food is eaten, such as breakfast, lunch, or dinner.

Bye~ (Low) Confidence: The feeling or belief that one cannot rely on someone or themselves, firm trust.
- the state of feeling uncertain about the truth of something.

Mealtimes should be a time where you are together with your family or friends. Let's be real; cooking at home saves your parents money. If you're looking for a great way to bond with someone, cooking might be the answer. You might think cooking isn't your specialty, but maybe you'll discover something new about yourself.

Having low confidence is a matter that can be changed, but it's not realistic to think you'll have all the confidence you need in one day. Low confidence can make you feel down about yourself. People may try to tell you that you're smart, beautiful, or kind towards others but if your self-confidence is low, you'll probably convince yourself otherwise.

Your confidence can be decreased not only by yourself but by other people too. Do you realize your words can crush people by saying hateful, jealous comments? It's ridiculous how people don't care about other people's feelings.

Chef Drake~

Drake has always had low confidence in himself. Back in the 2nd grade, he broke his wrist while playing on the monkey bars. He had to wear an arm cast for 6 weeks. His classmates wanted him to get better soon. They'd ask to sign their names to his cast to cheer him up, especially since he couldn't swing across the monkey bars at recess. His best friend, TJ would sit with him at recess every day and talk to him about things like football, cars, and famous basketball players.

Sadly, other students didn't treat Drake the same way. The biggest school bully, Ayden, would tell him that he wishes that he broke his other wrist too. He would push Drake into the lockers, trying to make him cry. Other students would just ignore him, whisper about his arm, and call him hurtful nicknames. Most of the teachers saw what was happening to

Drake, but they never did anything to end the bullying.

Sometimes, he would come home crying to his parents. His parents would come to the school, speak with the teachers & the principal, but they always said, "Well, we can't do anything about it because we can't stop the students from having their own opinion and comments about Drake's wrist. Sorry." His parents got upset every time they would use that tired, old excuse.

After the 2nd grade, his parents transferred him to a new school. The atmosphere was much better for him, but he always thought about the hateful comments he received back at his old school.

At 11 years old, he still has low confidence. Even though he played soccer, he would always convince himself that everyone was laughing at him. However, that wasn't the truth. All of his teammates congratulated him on the different awards he received, and everyone said he was the best player on the soccer team. Drake just couldn't bring himself to believe them. He thought they were saying all these encouraging comments about him just to be nice.

When at home, he loved watching Gordon Ramsey, Tasty, Jamie Oliver, Sunny Anderson, B. Smith, and many more talented chefs. He dreamed of going to culinary school, owning multiple restaurants, earning a Michelin star, and becoming a world-famous chef.

His mom saw how much Drake wanted to become a chef, but she also wanted him to build up his self-confidence. So, she decided to sign him up for cooking classes. Drake was very anxious and nervous about the idea, but after he got the hang of it, he loved it.

The cooking instructor and his parents were extremely proud of him. Ever since then, his confidence went through the roof. At school, he became popular, joined the cooking club, and even was asked to tutor other students. Low confidence isn't the easiest problem to fix. It takes *time and patience* for sure, but it's possible with the right tools.

For some people, confidence is something they've always had. They never went through being shy or convincing themselves of something they're not. Other people, however, do have to put in the effort to gain confidence in themselves. Find your squad that will always support you and stick with you, no matter what you're dealing with.

Recipes:

_____

_____

_____

_____

_____

_____

_____

_____

_____

_____

_____

Ch. 4- Giving Back + Being Arrogant

Hi~ Giving Back: Providing love or other emotional support; caring

Bye~ Arrogance: Having or revealing an exaggerated sense of one's importance or abilities

It is better to give than to receive, which is one of life's golden rules. Giving back will make you feel better about yourself while helping someone or making someone feel special. People appreciate and like other people who like to give back to others or their community.

No one desires to be around an arrogant person. Don't get me wrong, it's important and great to have confidence in yourself, but when you speak about yourself boastfully, that's not acceptable. Imagine your best friend or your favorite cousin being arrogant all the time. They're not humble and all they talk about is how amazing they are, that would be annoying.

The Same but Different~

Identical twins, Aaron and Aamir, who are 8, have completely different personalities. Aamir was shy, likes playing instruments, like the saxophone, kind, and loves to give back to his family, friends, and his community. Aaron on the other hand, was outgoing, loves playing sports, was arrogant, only liked receiving gifts, and he only thought about himself.

At school, Aaron would never let his friends talk about their weekend, or what they got on their science test. He just blabbered about all of his achievements, his grades, and never considered his friends. Sadly, he lost some of his friends, but Aaron never cared if he lost his friends, as long as he got to play sports and continue to receive gifts and compliments.

Aamir on the other hand loved to listen to his friends and teachers share about their weekends. He always offered to let someone be first in the student line or share some of his lunch with someone who didn't have lunch. Aamir believed that it feels better to give than receive. He was selfless, and people loved that quality about him.

Everyone, including the twin's parents, family, and close friends could see the difference between the two of them. Aaron didn't see anything wrong with his behavior. He believed it was okay to always put himself above everyone else. Aaron ignored his parent's advice when they suggested he give something away or let someone talk about their day.

Aamir tries to help Aaron with his arrogance, but Aaron is the type of person who thinks he's fine just the way he is. Aamir prayed every day that Aaron's actions, mood, and attitude would be the way the Lord desires it to be. Aamir had faith that God's plan would come at the right time, but he'll have to wait and trust in the Lord.

His parents, Pam and Anthony, also prayed for Aaron. They tried to discipline him, bribe him with toys & candy to change his ways, but nothing worked.

Well, after 2 years of trusting in God, hoping this time would come sooner than later, their prayer was answered. It was pizza Friday at Aamir & Aaron's school, and out of nowhere, Aaron asked one of his friends, Sam, how he was doing. Sam was expecting Aaron to yet again, talk about himself. He was very surprised at Aaron's sudden change of attitude & manners.

Even their English teacher noticed, so much so that she decided to allow the whole class to play outside, and best of all, no homework for the weekend.

Aamir was extremely happy for his twin brother. He was so grateful he trusted in the Lord, and that he had faith. When their parents heard the news, they screamed and jumped and ran and shouted in excitement.

They took the twins to their favorite ice cream shop and trampoline park with a bunch of their friends. Aaron felt awful for the way he was treating everyone. After a few days, Aaron decided to apologize to everyone he was being selfish and disrespectful towards. They forgave him and were proud of him for admitting his mistakes & taking responsibility for his actions.

Giving back goes a long way in life. Eventually, in life, the favor will be given back to you. You'll feel proud of yourself when you do something helpful for someone less fortunate or the community. People love a selfless person who puts others' needs before themselves. It's truly a wonderful quality to have.

Places to volunteer, items to donate; ways to give back:

_____

_____

_____

_____

_____

_____

_____

_____

_____

_____

Ch 5. - Reading + Fake Friends

Hi~ Reading: The action or skill of reading written or printed matter silently or aloud.

- an occasion at which poetry or other pieces of literature are read aloud to an audience.

Bye~ Fake Friends: (adj) not genuine; counterfeit.

- (noun) a thing that is not genuine, a forgery or sham.

Reading can get your imagination working. Even if this means you have to read it over and over again. Hopefully, you'll learn something new each time. When you're reading, it could give you a feeling of relaxation and calmness.

Have you ever had a so-called "friend" who didn't have your back in a certain situation? Maybe you invited them to your birthday party and they said that they would come, but they never showed? Do they rarely show up for multiple occasions? If so, they quite possibly may be a fake friend. They're people who trick you and waste your time. It's better to have a few REAL friends than to have many friends who don't have your best interest at heart.

What about your Friends~

A beautiful young woman named Imani went to Spelman College which is an all-girl HBCU (Historical Black Colleges and Universities). She has always been an introvert, never liked being at large parties or events. She had some trouble making friends in her childhood, yet Imani was determined to make some friends since none of her friends from high school were attending Spelman.

Her parents are extremely wealthy. Her mother has been a lawyer for 12 years, and her father has been an investment banker for 16 years. They were very happy when Imani wanted to attend Spelman because she always talked about attending her whole childhood.

The first day rolls around, Imani is super excited. She has her hair done, nails painted with a cute design, and has the perfect outfit for that added boost of confidence. Imani promised herself to get out of her comfort zone and make as many friends as she could. When she arrives at her first class, she sees three young ladies, all sitting next to each other.

Her body didn't want to sit with them, but she had to. She needed to be included in groups and get invited to parties around campus.

With some hesitation, she went over and introduced herself to them. The girls, Nya, Jayla, and Simone all wanted to be friends with Imani. They all had the same classes at the same time, so they were together all the time. They loved to study together. They would also help one another anytime they had sleepovers. They made TikToks and would laugh until their stomachs hurt. Imani was glad she chose to push herself to make friends.... it was amazing!

After the first semester and final exams, they all went home for Christmas. Nya's family lived an hour away, Jayla was from Chicago, and Simone's family lived in New York. During winter break, they all stayed in contact as much as they could.

As the second semester rolled around, Imani found out some news from Simone. "Imani, Nya, and Jayla were only friends with you because you're rich and they wanted to be popular off of your wealth."

They never really liked Imani. Simone told Imani, "Jayla was the one who didn't like you from the jump. When Nya heard Jayla's plan to use you, she didn't like the idea, and Nya really wanted to be friends with you. Jayla threatened Nya if she didn't agree and do what she said, Jayla would get revenge. So, Nya went along with it. "

Imani was furious and hurt. She was unsure if she should be angry at Nya because she sees her dilemma & why she made that choice, but at the same time, Imani believes she should've stood up for herself.

After a few weeks, she forgave Nya and Imani discovered a hobby that helped her heal from Jayla's disgraceful actions: reading.

Imani hasn't ever been a person who enjoys reading or is a person who reads daily, but she wanted to get in the habit of reading more often. The book she decided on was, The Hate U Give, by Angie Thomas. After the first few chapters, Imani instantly fell in love with reading.

She'd stock up on books she knew she would read. However, she didn't want to love reading by herself, so she introduced her love for books to Simone. After a few months, Imani and Simone formed a book club. They found people who wished to be part of a club that fits them, and a reading club was the answer.

Some may be view reading as boring, but to many people out there in the world, reading is everything. It's their favorite hobby, their love, the foundation of their imagination. Reading could also be something you focus on instead of fake people just like Imani.

Don't focus on people who waste your time. Friends come and go, but your best friends stay with you forever, like a good book.

List a few good books you'd like to read:

_____

_____

_____

_____

_____

_____

_____

_____

_____

_____

_____

Ch 6. - Be Yourself + Failure

Hi~ Be Yourself: Act naturally, according to one's character and instincts

Bye~ Failure: Lack of success.
- an unsuccessful person, enterprise, or thing

To be honest, if you are trying to be like someone else, you're wasting time that you wish you hadn't. Being you is perfectly normal. You should love yourself just the way you are. Plus, people rather be around those who enjoy love being themself than someone who is trying to look like some model on the gram or something.

In life, you're going to fail sometimes. However, that doesn't mean you fail on purpose, or you do something without effort. It's a horrible habit to think if you fail at one hobby or job, it means you'll fail at everything else. Don't let yourself think that way because the more you say that to yourself, the more you'll start to believe it. You have to put trust into yourself before anyone else can. You're your #1 fan.

My First Love~

A young man, named Jamal Carter, was a 15-year-old teen whose dream was to be in the music industry. He'd been working his butt off by recording samples and demos to send in for opportunities. Jamal loved music ever since he was 8. He knew he wanted to be in the music industry, he admired Biggie Smalls, Tupac, Lauryn Hill, and many other fabulous, iconic artists.

One day, Jamal asked his mom if she could buy him a mic and a keyboard to create beats. Jamal and his mom weren't the wealthiest people, and they did struggle from time to time, but she did everything she could to provide her son the best life she possibly could. Without hesitation and a few days of thinking, she said yes. He was thrilled!

As soon as he got the mic and keyboard, he spent hours creating different melodies and beats. His mom loved seeing him do what he loved. Jamal was interested in other activities here and there, but he always fell back to music. His friends would invite him to play football in their backyard or go to the park to play HORSE, but he always said no. Because of that, a lot of his friends came and went, but Jamal had his mother's support no matter what.

On Jamal's 17th birthday, he received the most pre-eminent gift, his mom managed to get Jamal to perform at the biggest concert of the year, in downtown Chicago! He couldn't believe it, he jumped and shouted and screamed in joy. Jamal asked his mom how she did it, but she said that'll always be a secret.

After the birthday party, he went to his room to pick out the best beats and melody to play while he was performing. Although Jamal was a little anxious because he wasn't used to writing lyrics. Jamal wasn't sure what to do. However, he always knew he could ask Derrick and Kasey for some advice. Derrick was a person who could make up a song under pressure fast. And Kasey was always ready to give out some advice for her boy.

The day had finally come. Jamal was going to execute his talent to thousands of people. He hoped that nothing would go wrong. Once they arrived downtown, Jamal felt pumped, energetic, and ready to do what he loved. As he walked out onto the stage, his music was blasting through the speakers, people started to clap to the beat.

One person shouted, "This music is about to be off the hook dawg!"

Jamal was feeling himself, every sound in the beat played a different role. Jamal started to rap his song, swaying his head, bouncing around like no one was watching. Right in the middle of the song,

Jamal stuttered severely, but he reminded himself, the show must go on. In the end, as the lyrics and beats were fading away, a man walked out onto the stage and told Jamal he was going to get critiqued by 3 of the biggest artists out right now.

The judges were very famous entertainers. Jamal was speechless. He felt like the world was ending right underneath his feet since he thought he did so horribly. Unfortunately, the judges agreed with his thoughts. No one knew about this but, if all 3 judges had given him at least a 7/10, one of them would become his vocal coach. Jamal was so disappointed and furious at himself.

When Jamal and his mother got back home, he threw away all of his music equipment. He began crying horribly. He locked himself in his room for several hours. His mom was beyond sad and worried for Jamal. She tried to help him cope and told him he shouldn't give up, to keep his head high like a boss, but it didn't help.

The next day, Jamal came to school with a crowd of people laughing at him because his performance went viral the night before. He felt humiliated. Derrick and Kasey wanted to help Jamal the best way they knew how, but Jamal was so stubborn and sad that he didn't want to open up to them. Throughout the day, he thought about finding a new interest like basketball. People always told him he had the height and body type for it, so he decided to give it a try.

At school, Jamal tried out for the basketball team, he made the squad and was actually pretty good. Jamal was feeling the satisfaction that came along with being a good player. Although he was also happy that no one was giving him weird glares in the hallway, he knew that basketball wasn't him. Jamal wanted to go back to his first love, music. However, was he ready for the critique from his peers? Or was he ready to overcome his emotions and give music a second chance?

Jamal opened up to his mom about how he was coping and what he was thinking. He needed her advice. She told him to follow his heart and trust his gut.

After some deep consideration, Jamal chose to be himself. He knew there were gonna be others' opinions, but he didn't care. He had all of the support he needed: his mom and his two best friends. He had to prove you can take a fall and get back up. His mom gave Jamal a surprise, his old music equipment. She couldn't let his music stuff go, so she kept it hidden from him until he was ready to come back to his true love.

Several months passed by and Jamal was loved by everyone: people from his school, his neighborhood, and across the country. He started a YouTube channel where he shared his passion to encourage others to be comfortable with following what they loved to do.

Eventually, his videos went viral and Jamal landed a huge contract where he would make 30k a month by making beats for major artists, and after a while, he released his very first song. People went crazy over it, his song made the top 100's list, received a Grammy, he was living his best life. There were haters out there, but that didn't stop him. As a token of appreciation, he bought his mom a new house with everything she loved, he bought Derrick a new car, and he bought Kasey a ticket to a place she has dreamed about going to for the longest time: Dubai.

Jamal became a very successful person by learning from his mistakes, being himself, and following his heart. You might choose the wrong door: failure. You might choose the right door: success. When you do something, you don't love but you're only doing it for people to like you, then you can't be truly happy. Do what makes you happy, no matter what.

Anything is possible with the right mindset, you have to be yourself because if you are, you will be something you don't want to miss out on. Failure shouldn't affect who you are because if it does, you'll have to do some soul-searching, and figure out what the best solution is for you.

Being yourself is so much fun!

Ch 7. - Create Something New + Loneliness

Hi~ Creating: Bring (something) into existence

Bye~ Loneliness: Sadness because one has no friends or company
- the fact of being without companions; solitariness.

Creating something new could mean writing a book or forming a book club. Don't do it for fame or money, do it because brings you joy, and enjoy the process along the way.

Loneliness is something you don't want to have. Nothing's wrong with wanting to be alone, but you shouldn't be in a little corner by yourself. Include yourself in activities, like clubs, parties, study groups, sports, and whatever occasions come up, attend to them.

Rags to Riches~

A young man, Brandon, was homeless and lonely. His parents passed away when he was 8 years old, and Brandon was an only child. Throughout his childhood, he got placed in multiple foster homes, and each family neglected him or verbally abused him, worse than the previous family. He didn't show emotions or tell anyone how he was handling the verbal abuse he faced.

When Brandon was in high school, he never participated in any sports or clubs. His teachers would ask him why, and he gave the same answer to each teacher, "I'm a shy person, and I'm not good at anything." His friends would try to get him into basketball or get him to come to a few parties, but Brandon refused. Eventually, they gave up on him, and they didn't want to be friends with him anymore. At one point, a girl, Ashley asked Brandon out to homecoming because she had the biggest crush on him for weeks. I mean, she had the most beautiful smile with her green eyes and wore the cutest reading glasses.

However, Brandon said no. He made up some excuse that he needed to attend a funeral that he couldn't avoid, even though he had no family. Since then, no girl wanted to be with him for not taking a chance.

After high school, Brandon didn't have any money for college, nowhere to crash, so, he ended up homeless. He would struggle to buy the necessities: food, water, clothing. He tried to apply for a job at different restaurants, stores, whatever he could find, but the store would deny him because of his appearance. Brandon owned no nice clothes for an interview, so as soon as he walked in, they told him no. After some time, Brandon stopped, looking for a job, and had to think of another way to make a living.

After 1 year of living in a shelter, Brandon thought of a plan: he would start a YouTube channel. Although he didn't have the equipment to film and edit with, he was able to use a camera from the shelter, which he would use from time to time. Brandon decided to film himself, talking about his childhood. To Brandon, it wasn't going to be easy for him to do because he feared people would make fun of him, say hurtful things which could hit close to home, but for him, this was the only option left. However, before he started filming, he did some research on how to edit and upload a video on YouTube.

The next day, Brandon had all the details he needed to make his video. He felt like starting a YouTube channel could open a new chapter. He wanted a fresh start, but he was afraid that the idea might not help, and he'll be back to square one. Brandon spent days thinking about filming the video, and he prayed about it, asking God what he should do. One night, while Brandon was sleeping, he had a dream where an angel appeared, dressed in all white. The angel said in the dream, "Follow your heart and you'll know the answer." When Brandon woke up in the morning, he had his answer: make the video. He set the camera in a place with good lighting, made sure no people were around, and he took some deep breaths.

Brandon struggled with making the intro. He kept on tearing up about the struggles he went through. However, after some very long hours, Brandon did it with pride. There was a lot of crying and vulnerability, but he did what he had to do. Right afterward, Brandon started to edit, cutting out the mistakes, using different filters to brighten his video, checking the audio, and everything.

He wasn't ready to post the same day, so he chose to wait a few days. That same night, when he went off to sleep, Brandon had the same dream with the same angel in it. The angel, told him the same message, "Follow your heart and you'll know the answer." So, Brandon followed his heart, and the next morning, he uploaded the video. A few hours had passed, but no one had seen or liked the video. Brandon knew he couldn't delete the video because God had plans for him, and he knew God wouldn't put him through a situation he couldn't handle. He kept his faith and waited patiently.

Brandon checked the video again. It had 30K views and 1,000 comments. Each comment said a kind word towards him. He jumped and screamed joy, knowing God was good. Not long after the success of Brandon's video, he met a man, who had been looking for him. He offered Brandon an opportunity to turn his story into a movie. Brandon couldn't believe it, this was really happening, his life was changing.

Within 9 months, Brandon's life had changed. He was now living in a new house and able to afford a car that allows him to volunteer at the shelter even after his newfound success. Brandon was happy and he loved being in front of the camera. He wanted to make more videos about his childhood, life updates, inner peace, vlogs, and more.

Over time, his subscribers grew rapidly; he now had 700k subscribers. Brandon had never been so happy in his life, and he thanked God every day. God created a new path for Brandon, he trusted God, followed the path, worked hard, and now, he's where he wanted to be.

Creating something new can lead you onto a path of success. You don't have to create something new for money or fame. You can do it for fun, and if it brings joy to you, that's the only thing that matters.

Being lonely isn't the life you want either, having people check up on you, making sure you are doing alright. Having alone time to yourself and being lonely are 2 different things. You should want a life full of fun and memories with the ones you loved the most.

Ch 8- Journaling + Overwhelmed

Hi~ Journaling: Writing in a journal or diary

Bye~ Overwhelming: Bury or drown beneath a huge mass

Journaling is healthy. It's where you get to write down your thoughts, your dreams, your goals, anything you want. You feel relieved when you pour everything out on paper if you're not comfortable with talking to someone.

Being overwhelmed usually means you're exhausted or worried. It's kind of like anxiety. It takes time to recover, and the process isn't easy. You must take baby steps. Sometimes, you can feel like you're defeated mentally, physically, emotionally, financially, and spiritually. I know trying to not feel overwhelmed can be a challenge for some people, but it can be done with determination, confidence, and consistency.

This time, the story is about me. I, Nyla Barnes, am a very outgoing, intelligent, a positive teenager, but like every person, I've had ups and downs throughout my life. A lot happened in my life before I started to journal daily. Before this and that happened, I would say my childhood was very peaceful, had lots of warmth, love, compassion, a normal life.

Fast forward to my 4th-grade year, I remember the day my mom told me my best friend, Trinity, was moving to a new school, I felt overwhelmed. Who would be my best friends who would I laugh with, play with? I met Trinity in the 2nd grade. She was shadowing my school for a day, and my 2nd-grade teacher, Mrs. Rudolph, told her to sit with me because I am a very kind person. I was thankful for that because that day, we clicked. We played and laughed together, and the next day, I was praying that she would come to my school.

As 3rd grade rolled in, Trinity came to my school with this great big smile on her face, and throughout the year, we were inseparable! So how was I to cope in 4th grade? Well, I did and made other great friends, and Trinity and I are still friends to this day, thanks to our moms for keeping in touch.

I have stayed in the hospitals 2 times in my life, and let's just say, they weren't very enjoyable. The 1st time I went to the hospital was back when I was around 5 years old. I had a stomach virus, and you might think, "Oh, so you stayed in the hospital for a day or two, right?"

Well, the answer is no. I stayed for A WHOLE WEEK. Also, the stomach virus was so severe that I had to get a blood transfusion (basically means I received someone's blood to replace my own blood).

Another time I stayed in the hospital was back in February of 2019. I had walking pneumonia. Basically, there was a cloud or build-up in my lungs which caused me to have a terrible cough, a high fever, my body was quite sore (especially my back), and I had to stay in the hospital for a whole week again. Those 2 experiences had me realize that I need to take care of my body more with urgency and love.

However, within all those times of being overwhelmed, I was struggling to find joy.

I didn't know how to express how I felt about certain occurrences. That's when journaling came into play for me. Journaling helped me a lot because it allowed me to let out my emotions without having to speak to anyone. It brought a wave of peace and a relaxed setting to my mind. I would write about my day, the ups, the downs, the good, the bad.

Journaling is a tool for whoever wants to use it. For me, it's the best healing mechanism because it's just writing. Also, I view journaling as writing about all of my memories with my family, my friends, dreams, vacations, and events I never want to forget. For example, when I went to California for the first time in the summer of 2021, I journaled about everything because it was one of the best vacations I've ever been on.

So, journaling might be the answer for you, or it may not be, and that's okay. No matter what you're going through, always keep your head up and have faith because it could be a blessing in disguise.

Special thanks to my GranCe who has gifted me with journals over the years.

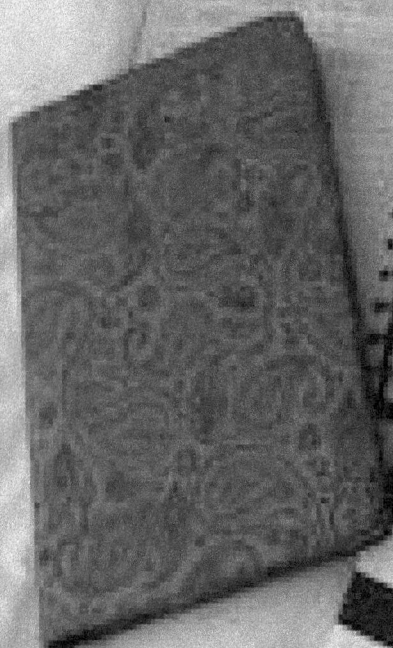